I love quizzes – though I'm not actually very good at them. I take part in a local fun quiz every Monday with my friends Joan, Gerry and Tony. I don't think we've ever won! I'm a pretty useless team member because I don't know anything about Sport or Geography or Pop Music. I'm not even very good at General Knowledge. I only seem to have *Specific* Knowledge! Sometimes Dave the Quiz Master decides to be very kind to me and includes a quiz round on Children's Literature, so I can get a chance to shine. Maybe I'll give him a copy of this super special Jacqueline Wilson Quiz Book.

I hope you'll have fun with the quizzes. I wonder if anyone will be able to answer every single question correctly? Don't worry if you can't remember the answers. I've got stuck on heaps of them myself, and yet I wrote the books! Here's a question I hope *everyone* can answer. Which author is so proud and pleased she has such lovely loyal fans? You've got it! ME!

Love from

Jacqueline Wilson

x x x

www.jacquelinewilson.co.uk

**Also available by award-winning
author, Jacqueline Wilson**

The Jacqueline Wilson QUIZ BOOK

Illustrated by
Nick Sharratt

THE JACQUELINE WILSON QUIZ BOOK
A CORGI YEARLING BOOK : 0 440 866 634

Published in Great Britain by Corgi Yearling Books,
an imprint of Random House Children's Books

First edition published 2002 exclusively for W H Smith
This edition published 2005 exclusively for W H Smith

1 3 5 7 9 10 8 6 4 2

Corgi Yearling Books are published by Random House Children's Books,
61–63 Uxbridge Road, London W5 5SA,
a division of The Random House Group Ltd,
in Australia by Random House Australia (Pty) Ltd,
20 Alfred Street, Milsons Point, Sydney, NSW 2061, Australia,
in New Zealand by Random House New Zealand Ltd,
18 Poland Road, Glenfield, Auckland 10, New Zealand,
and in South Africa by Random House (Pty) Ltd,
Endulini, 5A Jubilee Road, Parktown 2193, South Africa

THE RANDOM HOUSE GROUP Limited Reg. No. 954009
www.**kids**at**randomhouse**.co.uk

CONTENTS

Hold Your Own Jacqueline Wilson Quiz Night!

Why not make a special occasion of it? Get your best friends and fellow Jacqueline Wilson fans together for an ultra-tricky, mega-fun night of quizzing! Here are a few ideas for how to make the most of it.

Build Up Your Brain Power!

You will need:

- a helpful parent/guardian to take you all out for a good supply of brain food in advance of your Quiz Night (recommended menu: large burgers, French fries, and several jumbo-sized Cokes or strawberry milkshakes, followed by large ice-cream sundaes, butterscotch or chocolate flavour preferred).

Set the Scene

You might like to:

- choose a bedroom well away from any adults, so that the grown-ups can't hear what's going on
- close the curtains and decorate the room with silver stars and moons just like Tracy Beaker's bedroom in *The Dare Game*
- dress up as your favourite Jacqueline Wilson character (but if you choose Ruby from *Double Act* – DON'T CUT OFF ALL YOUR HAIR!)

Refreshments

The following items will create the right vibe:

- a large quantity of Smarties (for snacking and applying as lipstick)
- several bags of Hula Hoops (for snacking and wearing as rings)

- a good supply of fairy cakes with appropriate messages iced on top (e.g. *Clever Dick, Bird Brain, Champ, Chump* etc.) for prizes.

And Now for the Quiz!

Choose whichever of these items you think will help to make your Quiz Night run smoothly:

- a reliable Quiz Master who is also good at sums (to ask the questions without cheating, and to add up the scores without mistakes!)
- a Mickey Mouse alarm clock for setting a time limit
- a lucky mascot (e.g. a toy rabbit or a knitted robin)
- sparkly pens and notepads (for answers/scoring)
- a set of rainbow felt-tip pens (for optional tattoos while you're waiting for your next quiz question)
- And don't forget one copy of *The Jacqueline Wilson Quiz Book!*

Remember, you can use the quizzes in whichever order you like. You don't have to do them in the order they are set out in the book; and you don't have to do all twenty quizzes in the same session!

Scoring and Prizes

- Score one point per correct answer (and two points per correct answer in the Extra-tricky Quiz for Truly Dedicated Fans)
- Award fairy cakes or something of your own choice as prizes

And afterwards:

- Have one or two videos at the ready for late-night sleepover activity, after the quiz is finished (recommended titles: *The Wizard of Oz* or *The Railway Children* – NOT *The Monster!*)

Good luck!

Teasing Tests
on Your Top Titles

Quizzes 1–9

Pit your wits, tease your brain and see how much
you can remember from nine of the best books by
Jacqueline Wilson. But above all – have FUN!

Quiz 1
THE ILLUSTRATED MUM

1. When the story begins, it is Marigold's birthday; how old is she?

2. Why does Marigold think that her birthday tattoo ought to be in the shape of a cross?

3. What is the name of the Westwards' disagreeable neighbour downstairs in the basement flat?

4. Which Year is Star in at school?

5. What is the name of the school bully in Dolphin's class?

6. After Marigold finally returns after her birthday night out, what is she doing when Dolphin and Star get home from school?

7. What excuse does Tasha's mother give for refusing Marigold's invitation to tea?

8. What does Marigold have tattooed round her left ankle?

9. When Dolphin and Marigold walk down to Beech Brook, what do they do with all the cakes they have with them?

10. What colour are Marigold's eyes?

11. What is Kayleigh Richards' nickname for Dolphin at school?

12. What is Owly Morris's real name?

13. What surprise does Marigold have in store for Star when she returns from the concert?

14. What type of creature does Marigold choose at the big toyshop in London?

15. How does Marigold pay for her train ticket to Brighton?

16. What is Dolphin's comfort object, which she takes to bed with her when she's feeling upset?

17. Why does Dolphin smash the mobile phone?

18. How does Star manage to make contact after Dolphin has broken the mobile phone?

19. Why does Dolphin call for an ambulance?

The Full Picture

20. How did Marigold meet Dolphin's father?

Quiz 2
DOUBLE ACT

1   Which of the twins, Ruby or Garnet, is the elder, and by how much?

2. What inspires the twins to write their life story?

3. What awful experience did Garnet have during the Infants' nativity play?

4. What happens to Gran after Dad is made redundant?

5. What does the twins' dad decide to do after he loses his job?

6. What does Rose do for a living when she first meets the twins' dad?

7. What do Ruby and Garnet call their special language?

8. Something unfortunate happens to Rose in the van: what is it?

9. What is Garnet's favourite film of all time?

10. What is the name of Dad's new venture?

11. What does Ruby do when the Blob puts a wriggly worm down her jumper?

12. What sort of creature does Ruby choose for the Noah's Ark painting on the classroom wall?

13. Why is Garnet surprised by Ruby's choice of creature?

14. How does Ruby raise the money to pay for the twins' train tickets to London?

15. Who turns up just at the wrong moment, during Ruby and Garnet's audition?

16. What is the title of the essay in Ruby and Garnet's entrance exam?

17. What is the name of Gran's new gentleman friend?

18. What is the Blob's nickname for Ruby after she cuts her hair off?

19. What is Dad's nickname for Ruby after she cuts her hair off?

20. What does Rose cook on Garnet's last night at home before term begins?

Quiz 3
THE STORY OF TRACY BEAKER

1   When is Tracy Beaker's birthday?

2. Who shares the same birthday with Tracy at the Home?

3. What is the name of the pet rabbit at the Home?

4. Why was Tracy taken into care?

5. What is Tracy's name for her social worker?

6. Who are Tracy's first foster parents?

7. What happens to Bluebell?

8. What happened when Tracy tried to visit her mum in Watford?

9. Why do Julie and Ted decide to give up fostering Tracy?

10. Why does Cam Lawson first visit the Children's Home?

11. Who is Tracy's best friend at the Home, before Justine Littlewood comes along?

12. What is the first thing Tracy dares Justine Littlewood to do?

13. What does Justine Littlewood dare Tracy to do in return?

14. What is the Quiet Room?

15. What excuse does Tracy always use to cover up the fact that she has been crying?

16. What is the name of Tracy's goblin character which she uses to illustrate one of her letters to Cam Lawson?

17. What unwelcome surprise is in store for Tracy, just when she is starting to be properly friendly with Peter Ingham?

18. What suggestion does Tracy put to Cam Lawson when they are having lunch together in McDonald's?

19. What special present does Cam give Tracy?

20. What does Tracy do with Cam's present?

Quiz 4
THE SUITCASE KID

1   Where did Andy live before her parents split up?

2. What do Katie's *Care Bears* video cases *really* contain?

3. How did Andy's mum meet Bill the Baboon?

4. How many children does Bill have, and what are their names?

5. Where does Andy go when she wants some peace and quiet in the house?

6. When Andy's dad says that she should choose the name for Carrie's unborn baby, what is Andy's first suggestion?

7. What is special about the garden in Larkspur Lane?

8. What is the proper name for the little Japanese poems that Andy learns about at school?

9. Why is Katie scared of going to sleep?

10. What happens to Radish in the garden at Larkspur Lane?

11. Why does Andy run away from the garden?

12. Where does Andy end up the night she goes out to rescue Radish?

13. In Andy's dream, what does the wording say inside the pink teacup that Dad gives to Mum as a present?

14. What colour was the front door at Andy's old house?

15. What colour is the front door now?

16. When Andy finds Radish, what surprise awaits her?

17. What are the elderly lady and gentleman called?

18. What does the elderly lady give Andy for Christmas?

19. What does Katie give Andy for Christmas?

20. What is Radish's best Christmas present ever?

Quiz 5
THE LOTTIE PROJECT

1 What do Charlie's initials (C.A.K.E.) stand for?

2. Why won't Miss Beckworth allow Charlie to sit next to her special friends?

3. Which topic does Charlie choose for her Victorian project?

4. Name the class swot who sits next to Charlie at school.

5. Where does the class swot live?

Ooh! please Miss Beckworth!

6. What is Jo's job, until she is made redundant?

7. What is Jo and Charlie's favourite imaginary game called?

8. In Charlie's Victorian project, what is Lottie's job?

9. What is shocking to Charlie about Jo's cleaning job at the big house?

10. When Charlie and her friends started up a club at school the previous year, what did the initials GAB stand for on the club badge?

11 Why does Grandma invite Jo and Charlie round for a special Sunday lunch?

12. What is Charlie's special present for her grandparents, and why does it turn out to be a disappointment after all her efforts?

13. What is Jo really doing when she tells Charlie that she is babysitting Robin while Mark goes out?

Robin

14. Where does Mark take Jo, Charlie and Robin on their Sunday outing together?

15. Where had Mrs Edwards invited Charlie to go on the same day?

16. What happens during the Stardust Sparkle ride?

17. Why does Mark ring up Jo at three o'clock in the morning?

18. What does the police officer find by the duckpond?

19. What happens to baby Freddie in Charlie's Victorian diary?

20. To whom does Charlie unexpectedly blurt out all her troubles?

Quiz 6
THE BED AND BREAKFAST STAR

1   Why did Elsa's mum name her 'Elsa'?

2. What is Elsa famous for (a habit which drives nearly everyone up the wall!)?

3. Where do Elsa's family live when they are in Scotland?

4. Name the bed-and-breakfast hotel that Elsa and her family move into back in England.

5. Where do Elsa and Pippa meet Naomi, and what is she doing?

6. How many brothers does Naomi have?

7. Can you name Naomi's brothers?

8. Which room does Elsa's family occupy at the hotel?

9. According to Elsa, 'Where do baby apes sleep?'

10. What is unusual about Naomi's copy of *Little Women?*

11. What do the children call Mrs Macpherson, the cleaning lady?

12. What does Elsa get up to with her new black magic-marker pen?

13. What does Mack buy for a fiver at a car-boot sale?

14. What does Elsa tell the kids at school about her mum?

15. What does the manager tell Naomi's family after Naomi is interviewed by the television crew?

16. When Elsa wakes up in the middle of the night, what does she discover?

17. How does Elsa's loud voice come in useful that night?

18. What happens at first when Elsa gets her big chance to appear on national TV outside the hotel that night?

19. What is particularly appropriate about the jacket Elsa is given by the ladies in the church hall, after her family have lost all their possessions?

20. Where do Elsa's family move to after the bed-and-breakfast hotel?

Quiz 7
VICKY ANGEL

1 What do the other children at school call Vicky and Jade, and why?

2. What does Jade want to be when she grows up?

3. Where does Vicky's father work?

4. Who else, apart from Jade, thinks that she can see Vicky's ghost?

5. Where does Jade's family live?

6. On which day of the week did Vicky's accident happen?

7. Who does Jade find at the school gates on the next schoolday after the accident?

8. When the ghostly Vicky persuades Jade to bunk off school, where do they go?

9. What did Jade miss unknowingly when she bunked off school?

10. What is the title of Vicky's essay, which Jade reads out at the funeral?

11. What colour is Vicky's beautiful, long hair?

12. Why does Jade turn down Miss Gilmore's request that she join the Drama Club?

13. What does Mrs Cambridge catch Jade doing in the library?

14. What sort of help does Mrs Cambridge think Jade needs?

15. What unwelcome surprise does Jade's mum spring on her when they go to London for their 'girly day out'?

16. What surprise does Sam spring on Jade when Mr Lorrimer takes them up to Fairwood Park?

17. Who is Mrs Wainwright?

18. Why does Mrs Wainwright understand what Jade is going through?

19. Jade receives an official letter several weeks after the accident; what is it about?

20. Who saves Jade from being run over by a car, when she runs away?

Quiz 8
BAD GIRLS

1   Which of the school bullies is Mandy most afraid of?

2.   What happens to Mandy after her row with the bullies?

3.   What does Mandy like to collect as a hobby? (Clue: she has twenty-two of them!)

4.   Which of Mandy's classmates rings her at home to see if she is all right?

5.   What is Tanya's little sister called?

6. Which lesson is taking place when the three school bullies are summoned to see the headmistress?

7. Which book does Arthur King share with Mandy in the playground, when he is trying to protect her from the bullies?

8. What does Mandy see as she waits outside the newsagent's shop for Tanya?

9. Which board game does Arthur King try to interest Mandy in?

10. What does Mandy give Tanya as a present, after her shopping spree with her mum?

11. Where does Mandy's dad take her and Tanya on Sunday?

12. What does Tanya 'acquire' from Boots when she and Mandy go shopping?

13. What does Tanya draw, in felt-tip pen, on the inside of Mandy's wrist?

14. Where does Tanya have to move to when her foster mother feels she can no longer cope with her?

15. For which holiday activity does Mandy's mum sign her up, and where does it take place?

16. Who else has also signed up for this activity?

17. What is the shocking news that Mandy's mum receives at the end of that week?

18. What is the name of Mandy's new teacher in Year Six?

19. What is the subject for discussion during the class's first Circle Time?

20. What happens to Tanya after she's appeared in Court – and how does Mandy learn about it?

Quiz 9
SECRETS

1   Why does Treasure move in with her nan?

2. What do India and her mum constantly argue about?

3. What is the name of the only best friend that India has ever had?

4. What is India's favourite book?

5. What is Treasure's nickname at her latest school?

6. What is Treasure doing when she and India first meet?

7. Why is India walking home from school by herself that day?

8. What is the medical condition from which Treasure suffers?

9. What is Nan's proper name?

10. What is Wanda's secret, which is no secret to India?

11. What does India want to be when she grows up?

12. Which scary character does India meet when she goes round to see Treasure at her nan's flat?

13. Treasure has a special name for her diary; what does she call it?

14. What is Loretta's baby called?

15. Who helps Treasure to hide, when she is running away from Terry?

16. Where does India live?

17. What course of action does India suggest in order to help Treasure hide from the awful Terry?

18. What shocking development does India learn about when she goes round to Nan's flat to try and get Treasure's inhaler?

19. What is special about the picture Treasure has drawn in her 'attic' diary?

20. Who does India find in the kitchen when she goes downstairs for an early morning glass of milk?

Tricky Teasers on Jacqueline's Trivia!

Quizzes 10–20

Anything and Everything!

Battle with your brain cells on an assortment of themes which only have one thing in common – Jacqueline Wilson!

Quiz 10

Can You Place these Places?

1   In *Cliffhanger*, who lives at 10 Rainbow Street, Didcot?

2. In *Buried Alive!*, what is the name of the seaside town in Wales that Tim's family go to on holiday?

3. In *The Lottie Project*, where do the police eventually find Robin?

4. In *The Lottie Project*, where do Mark, Robin, Jo and Charlie go on their second, more successful, outing together?

5. In *The Lottie Project*, why is the Russell Coates Gallery of interest to Charlie?

6. In *The Illustrated Mum*, where does Star's father, Mickey, live?

7. In *The Illustrated Mum*, where does Marigold go to have her tattoos inked?

8. In *Secrets*, what is the name of the estate where Treasure lives?

9. In *Secrets*, which country does Wanda, the au pair, come from?

10. In *Secrets*, which city provides the background for Moya Upton's latest assignment, and whose famous house do India and Treasure visit?

11. In *The Suitcase Kid*, where do Andy's nan and grandad live?

12. In *The Bed and Breakfast Star*, why do Elsa and her family move to Scotland?

13. In *The Story of Tracy Beaker*, where does Tracy go to school?

14. In *The Dare Game*, where does Tracy persuade Cam to take her on their first trial weekend together before Cam becomes her foster mother?

15. In *The Dare Game*, where does Tracy go when she decides to start bunking off school?

16. In *The Dare Game*, where exactly is Alexander when he and Tracy first meet?

17. In *Vicky Angel*, where do Vicky's parents go to get away from it all, after Vicky's accident?

18. In *The Cat Mummy*, where does Verity eventually find Mabel?

19. Where does Rebecca first meet Glubbslyme the toad?

20. In *The Worry Website*, where does Samantha's dad go instead of coming over for her brother Simon's birthday, as he'd promised?

Quiz 11
All in the Family!

1 In *Double Act*, what was Ruby and Garnet's mum called?

2. In *Double Act*, what did Ruby and Garnet's gran do for a living before she retired?

3. In *The Suitcase Kid*, what is Andy's new baby half-sister called?

4. In *Secrets*, which famous young diary-writer from the Second World War does India think of as her 'soul sister'?

5. In *Secrets*, what is unusual about Treasure's aunt, Patsy?

6. In *Secrets*, why does a police car draw up outside India's house, after Treasure has come out of hiding?

7. In *Bad Girls*, why do Melanie, Sarah and Kim tease Mandy about her parents?

8. In *Bad Girls*, what happened to Tanya's mum?

9. In *The Worry Website*, how did Holly's dad meet his new girlfriend?

10. In *The Worry Website*, what is at the root of Samantha's worry?

11. In *The Story of Tracy Beaker*, what does Tracy tell Cam Lawson about her mother's job?

12. In *The Dare Game*, what is Tracy's real mum called?

13. In *The Dare Game*, what important news does Tracy's social worker have for her about her mum?

14. In *The Cat Mummy*, who did Mabel originally belong to?

15. In *The Cat Mummy*, why has Verity's dad printed loads of posters to pin to all the nearby trees, fences and lamp-posts?

16. In *The Cat Mummy*, why have all Gran's lavender bath salts disappeared?

17. In *The Illustrated Mum*, what are the names of Michael's wife and two daughters?

18. In *The Mum-Minder*, what does Gemma's mum do for a living?

19. In *Cliffhanger*, why does Tim's dad think that Tim has turned into 'a right Mummy's boy'?

20. In *Buried Alive!*, why does Tim's dad have to climb over the side of the pier?

Quiz 12

Clues to Clothes and More

1   In *Vicky Angel*, what is special about the ghostly Vicky's outfits when she appears to her best friend, Jade?

2. In *The Cat Mummy*, what does Verity wear after she realizes that all the clothes in her wardrobe are far too pongy to put on?

3. In *The Illustrated Mum*, what is different about Star's appearance when she returns from Brighton?

4. In *Double Act*, why does Ruby cut off her hair?

5. How does Glubbslyme dry Rebecca's dress after she's fallen in the pond?

6. What happens when Rebecca asks Glubbslyme to put a hex on horrible Mandy and her new shoes?

7. In *Secrets*, what does India's mother do for a living?

8. In *Secrets*, what nickname is given to India by Chris (the educational psychologist)?

9. In *The Story of Tracy Beaker*, how does Tracy prepare herself for Cam Lawson's first visit to the Children's Home?

10. In *The Story of Tracy Beaker*, what does Tracy specially notice about Cam Lawson's socks?

11. In *The Dare Game*, amongst the many presents that Tracy's mum buys her, there are two items of designer clothing; what are they?

12. In *Bad Girls*, how does Tanya acquire all her fashion accessories and make-up?

13. In *Bad Girls*, what colour is Tanya's hair when Mandy first meets her?

14. In *Bad Girls*, what is Indigo, and what happens while Tanya and Mandy are there?

15. In *Bad Girls*, what does Tanya give Mandy as a goodbye present, in exchange for Mandy's rainbow felt-tip pens?

16. In *The Worry Website*, why does Greg go 'all red and shuddery' when his class are trying on Victorian clothes during their school outing to the museum?

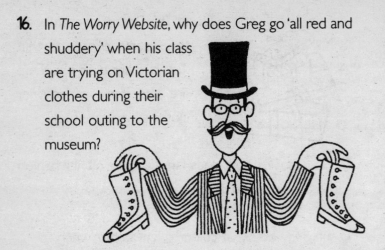

17. In *The Illustrated Mum*, what does Dolphin's witch dress look like?

18. In *The Bed and Breakfast Star*, what does Elsa wear to her mum's wedding to Mack the Smack, and why?

19. In *Cliffhanger*, what article of clothing does Tim's dad buy for him specially, so he'll look tough on his Adventure Holiday?

20. In *Buried Alive!*, what is it about Kelly's mum's boyfriend Dave that Tim and Biscuits think is pretty cool?

Quiz 13
Yum, Yum: All about Food!

1   In *The Mum-Minder*, what does Clive's mum give Sadie as a reward for helping to look after the children during their day at the chocolate shop?

2.   In *The Story of Tracy Beaker*, why is Tracy worried about going to McDonald's with Cam?

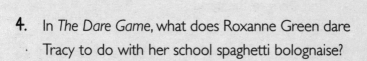

3.   In *The Story of Tracy Beaker*, what special treat does Cam buy Tracy for afternoon tea?

4.   In *The Dare Game*, what does Roxanne Green dare Tracy to do with her school spaghetti bolognaise?

5.   In *The Dare Game*, what refreshments has Alexander organized for himself at the house, before he meets Tracy for the first time?

6. In *The Dare Game*, what does Tracy tell Football about the ingredients of the meat loaf at her last Children's Home?

7. In *The Bed and Breakfast Star*, what does Elsa have for breakfast on her first morning at the hotel?

8. In *Glubbslyme*, name the tasty dish that Glubbslyme's witch used to cook for him in the seventeenth century.

9. How does Rebecca persuade Glubbslyme to take her flying in the park?

10. In *Glubbslyme*, what does Rebecca do in order to take the slug spell off Mandy?

11. In *The Worry Website*, what is the name of the eating competition that Mr Speed won when he was at school?

12. In *The Lottie Project*, what is the name of the cook in Charlie's Victorian diary?

13. In *The Lottie Project*, what is the message on the last cake that Charlie gives away in class, and who does she give it to?

14. In *The Lottie Project*, what special present does Charlie take to Robin in the hospital?

15. In *The Lottie Project*, what is the name of the magnificent Victorian cake that Charlie makes for the school disco?

16. In *The Cat Mummy*, Moyra offers to share her sweets with Verity at break-time; can you remember what sort they are?

17. In *Cliffhanger*, what does Biscuits have hidden up his sweatshirt which makes Tim think perhaps things aren't so bad after all?

18. In *Buried Alive!*, what is on the menu for supper at Kelly's caravan?

19. In *Buried Alive!*, what ice-cream mega-treat does Biscuits choose at the ice-cream parlour?

20. In *Secrets*, what is the name of the expensive Italian restaurant that India suggests she and her father go to for lunch (before she realizes that he has serious money problems)?

Quiz 14
Playing Games

1   In *Vicky Angel*, which after-school club does Vicky persuade her best friend, Jade, to join?

2. Can you name the teacher in charge of this club?

3. In *Vicky Angel*, where was Vicky's mother when she heard about the accident?

4. In *Cliffhanger*, in which team is Tim at the Adventure Centre?

5. In *Cliffhanger*, what is the proper name of Tim's cliffhanging activity?

6. In *Cliffhanger*, what happens to Kelly's purple-haired troll doll during the canoeing activity?

Theresa

7. In *Buried Alive!*, which beach game does Tim's dad keep wanting to play?

8. In *Buried Alive!*, what sort of sport does Biscuits like best, and why?

9. In *Buried Alive!*, what game does Biscuits play to get his own back on Tim?

10. In *The Illustrated Mum*, where does Dolphin's father, Michael, work?

11. In *The Story of Tracy Beaker*, what sort of games did Peter Ingham enjoy playing with his nan, before she died?

12. In *The Dare Game*, how does Tracy Beaker meet fellow truant, Football?

13. In *The Dare Game*, when Tracy's mum cancels their weekend together, saying that she has to meet a film producer, what is she really planning?

14. In *The Dare Game*, why does Football think all dads are rubbish?

15. In *The Worry Website*, how does Mr Speed suggest that Claire deals with her fear?

16. In *The Worry Website*, who is Claire's greatest sporting hero?

17. In *The Worry Website*, why did Samantha's parents have rows about her dad's sporting activities?

18. In The Suitcase Kid, what does Andy use to make a boat for Radish?

19. In The Lottie Project, what punishment does Miss Beckworth think up for Charlie, Lisa and Angela, when she discovers them hiding in the girls' toilets in order to avoid playing rounders?

20. What is Jacqueline Wilson's favourite sport?

Quiz 15
TV, Radio and the Theatre

1 Which book by Jacqueline Wilson has recently been serialized on CBBC1, and stars Dani Harmer in the title role?

2. Name the famous actress who co-directed the above series. (Clue: she made many appearances in Grange Hill and EastEnders!)

3. Jacqueline has recently appeared in a Channel 4 Television adaptation of one of her own books; do you know which one?

4. Which of Jacqueline's books was dramatized for the theatre in 1999?

5. Do you know which theatre staged this dramatization?

6. Where did Jacqueline come in Treasure Islands' Favourite Children's Author poll on BBC Radio Four?

7. When the BBC television programme, Bookworm, ran a poll to find the Nation's Favourite Children's Book, which of Jacqueline's titles featured in the top ten?

8. Which character from Jacqueline's books has her own page on the BBC website?

9. In *The Bed and Breakfast Star*, what is the name of the television programme being filmed in the foyer of the hotel?

10. Why does the director think that Elsa's interview is unsuitable?

11. In *The Bed and Breakfast Star*, which special television programme features Elsa's second interview later in the year?

12. In *Double Act*, for which children's television serial do Ruby and Garnet audition?

13. How do Ruby and Garnet's performances compare at the audition?

14. In *Double Act*, do you know at which boarding school the television serial is to be filmed?

15. In *The Story of Tracy Beaker*, Tracy imagines having her own chat show on TV when she grows up; what does she think it will be called?

16. In *The Dare Game*, which television programme is being 'broadcast' on Alexander's cardboard TV set?

17. In *The Dare Game*, Tracy tells Alexander and Football that her mum is somebody very famous; can you remember who?

18. In *Secrets*, what unpleasant surprise is in store for India and Treasure when they switch on India's portable television?

19. In *Secrets*, what is the name of the media campaign which is started up following Treasure's announcement that she wants to live with her nan, rather than her mum and stepdad?

20. In *The Worry Website*, what part does Natasha's wheelchair play in making Natasha and Lisa the 'glitter-girl stars' of the school concert?

Quiz 16
School Life

1. In *The Illustrated Mum*, who is the friendly librarian at Dolphin's school?

2. What sort of book does he pick out for Dolphin and Owly to look at?

3. In *Double Act*, who is Garnet's 'Sheepdog' at her new school, and what does it mean?

4. In *Double Act*, name the head teacher of the boarding school.

5. In *Secrets*, who is Tiffany?

6. In *Secrets*, why is India summoned to see the headmistress?

7. In *The Lottie Project*, what punishment does Miss Beckworth give Charlie for not sticking to the rules in her English exercise (the one about writing a formal letter of apology)?

8. In *The Lottie Project*, who wins the prize for the best project on the Victorians?

9. In *The Lottie Project*, who wins the prize for the best project on how it felt to be a Victorian?

10. In *The Cat Mummy*, what is the special topic being covered by Verity's class this term?

11. What is Verity's teacher called?

12. What does Verity's teacher suggest as a good way of remembering Mabel?

13. In *The Mum-Minder*, what is Sadie's homework for the half-term holiday?

14. In *The Dare Game*, why is Tracy Beaker summoned to see Mr Donne, the head teacher, at the beginning of the story?

15. In *The Dare Game*, what is Alexander's worst subject at school?

16. In *The Dare Game*, what does Alexander's father threaten to do if Alexander doesn't start standing up for himself at school?

17. In *The Dare Game*, what does Alexander's nickname become at school, after he takes Tracy's advice about dealing with the bullies in the showers?

18. Who had the original idea for *The Worry Website* on the classroom computer?

19. In *The Worry Website*, who used to be Holly's favourite teacher, and why isn't she any longer?

20. In *Bad Girls*, why does Mandy's mum go to see the headmistress, Mrs Edwards?

Quiz 17
What's in a Name?

1 In *Vicky Angel*, name
the boy in Jade's class
who tries to befriend her.

2. Why does Vicky want Jade
to start calling her 'Vicky Angel'?

3. In *The Cat Mummy*, Verity's best friend, Sophie, has
four kittens; what are their names?

4. In *The Cat Mummy*, what is the name of the golden
Labrador dog that belongs to Verity's friend, Laura?

5. In *The Cat Mummy*, what does Verity's name mean (clue: it comes from the Latin word *veritas*) and why does it suit her?

6. In *Cliffhanger*, what is the name of posh Giles's teddy bear?

7. In *Cliffhanger*, what is Biscuits' nickname for posh Giles?

8. In *Buried Alive!*, what do Tim and Biscuits call the two bullies on the beach behind their backs?

9. What do Tim and Biscuits call the main bully to his face?

10. In *Double Act*, what is the Blob's real name?

11. In *The Suitcase Kid*, what does Andy's stepsister, Katie, call her?

12. In *The Suitcase Kid*, what are Carrie's twins called?

13. In *Glubbslyme*, what is the name of the witch who was cast down into the pond during the seventeenth century?

14. In *Glubbslyme*, what is a *Bufo bufo*?

15. In *The Story of Tracy Beaker*, who is Bluebell?

16. In *The Dare Game*, how does Tracy refer to her current class teacher?

17. In *The Dare Game*, what does Cam call Tracy's bedroom after they've redecorated it?

18. In *Bad Girls*, who is Miranda Rainbow?

19. In *The Worry Website*, what is William's nickname at school, and why?

20. In *The Illustrated Mum*, what is Mark's nickname for Star when the gang hangs out at McDonald's?

Quiz 18
Everybody's Favourites

1 In *Vicky Angel*, what were Vicky's favourite flowers?

2. In *The Bed and Breakfast Star*, what is Pippa's favourite comfort object called?

3. In *The Bed and Breakfast Star*, who is Elsa's least favourite person of all time?

4. In *The Story of Tracy Beaker*, what is Tracy's favourite colour?

5. In *The Dare Game*, what is Tracy Beaker's favourite food in all the world?

6. In *The Dare Game*, what is Tracy's all-time favourite film?

7. In *The Dare Game*, what is Tracy's favourite girl's name, and why?

8. In *The Worry Website*, what is Holly's favourite fairy tale?

9. In *The Worry Website*, what is Claire's least favourite colour, and why?

10. In *Double Act*, what are Ruby and Garnet's favourite colours, and why?

11. In *Double Act*, what is Ruby's favourite subject at school?

12. In *Cliffhanger*, what is Tim's favourite sport?

13. In *The Illustrated Mum*, what flavour is Dolphin's favourite ice-cream sundae at McDonald's?

14. In *The Illustrated Mum*, what was the name of Micky's favourite band in the Eighties?

15. In *Bad Girls*, what is the name of Mandy's favourite toy.

16. In *The Suitcase Kid*, what is Andy's favourite-ever film?

17. In The Mum-Minder, what would be Sadie's least favourite job when she grows up?

18. In Glubbslyme, what are the toad's favourite sweets?

19. What is Jacqueline Wilson's favourite holiday destination, and why?

20. Whose favourite place for a break is Swaledale, in North Yorkshire? (Clue: he illustrates nearly all of Jacqueline's books!)

Quiz 19

Extra-tricky for Truly Dedicated Fans!

1 Name the popular illustrator of many of Jacqueline Wilson's books.

2. Which girls' magazine, popular in the Seventies, was named after Jacqueline Wilson?

3. Which two of Jacqueline's books boast two illustrators, and why?

4. What do Jacqueline Wilson and Treasure's nan (in *Secrets*) have in common? (Clue: think cowboy boots!)

5. Do you know where Jacqueline Wilson went to school?

6. How many fan letters do you think Jacqueline receives every week?

7. Jacqueline has also written a series of novels for adults: what subject links them all?

8. Which of Jacqueline's novels won the Guardian Children's Fiction Prize *and* the Children's Book of the Year Award in 2000?

9. In *The Story of Tracy Beaker*, Tracy is ten years and two months old when she begins to write My Book About Me. Can you work out which month it must be at the time of writing?
(Clue: think birthdays!)

10. What is Tracy Beaker's 'most Daring Dare ever'?

11. In *The Illustrated Mum*, what is the correct term for the condition from which Marigold suffers?

12. Whose motto is, 'Make friends, make friends, never never break friends'?

13. Who has rainbow glasses?

14. In *Double Act*, what is the name of the country village the twins move to?

15. Which village and county provide the location for the boarding school the twins want to attend?

16. In *Double Act*, why are china dolls a sensitive subject with Ruby?

17. In *The Lottie Project*, which famous Victorian novel does Charlie give to Jamie Edwards for Christmas, and why this one in particular?

18. The *Sunday Telegraph* described one of Jacqueline's stories as 'a complex and moving exploration of guilt and bereavement'; can you guess which one?

19. In *The Cat Mummy*, can you name the special cat goddess that Verity's class learn about as part of their project?

20. Can you remember the wording of the dedication at the beginning of *The Mum-Minder*?

Quiz 20
All about Jacqueline Wilson!

1   In which English city was Jacqueline Wilson born?

2. Where does she live now?

3. How old was Jacqueline when she wrote her first novel'?

4. How many brothers and sisters does she have?

5. Guess how many books Jacqueline has crammed into her house!

6. What are her favourite foods?

7. When is Jacqueline's birthday?

8. What is her star sign?

9. How many children does she have?

10. What are Jacqueline's favourite colours?

11. How many rings does she wear at any one time?

12. What did Jacqueline do for a living before she became a full-time author?

13. Which is Jacqueline's own favourite character in her books?

14. Can you name Jacqueline's favourite fictional character ever?

15. How many copies of Jacqueline's books do you think have been sold in the UK alone?

16. Jacqueline has written a series of books about the characters Ellie, Magda and Nadire; do you know what they are called?

17. What do Jacqueline and Andy – from *The Suitcase Kid* – have in common?

18. Which is the tidiest room in Jacqueline's house?

19. Which of Jacqueline's books has won the most awards?

20. Can you name the awards?

Cheaty Bits!

All About Jacqueline Wilson
A Brief Biography

Jacqueline Wilson was born in Bath, Somerset, just before Christmas on 17 December 1945. By the time she was six years old she had already decided that she wanted to become a writer, and by the age of nine had produced her first 'novel', filling up many Woolworths exercise books along the way!

After leaving school, Jacqueline worked as a journalist – and even had a teen magazine – Jackie – named after her! Since having her daughter, Emma, Jacqueline has been a full-time author, winning countless prestigious awards and selling millions of copies of her books in the UK alone. A number of her titles have also been adapted for television (most recently *The Story of Tracy Beaker* and *Double Act*) and dramatized for the theatre (*The Lottie Project*). She has also undertaken brilliantly successful book tours in Australia and New Zealand, proving that the appeal of her stories is truly worldwide!

Nowadays, when she isn't travelling up and down the country for signing sessions, Jacqueline lives in Kingston-upon-Thames, in Surrey. Her house overflows with books (15,000 at a rough guess!), pictures, dolls, ornamental elephants and a large family of teddy bears. Her hobbies are reading, going to art galleries and the cinema, swimming (fifty lengths before breakfast every morning), and line dancing. Jacqueline describes herself as 'small and skinny with very short, spiky hair and silver glasses'; she always wears black and doesn't feel fully dressed without a big, chunky ring on every finger! When asked what it's like being a famous writer, her reply is, 'It's WONDERFUL!'

Jacqueline's Favourites

Favourite food

Fruit – but cakes and chips when I'm feeling wicked

Favourite colour

Black and silver

Favourite sport

Swimming – I do fifty lengths in my local pool every morning

Favourite time of the day

Midnight – when I'm sitting up reading in bed

Favourite pen

A big ornate black and silver pen (a present from my daughter Emma)

Favourite place to go for a walk

Home Park – especially in the autumn when there are toadstools the size of dinner plates

Favourite animal

Lemur

Favourite book

Lavender's Blue, a nursery rhyme book illustrated by Harold Jones

Favourite smell

Roses

Favourite thing to wear

Black velvet

Favourite music

Queen, Anonymous 4, Dory Previn, Mary Chapin Carpenter, Renée Fleming, Michael Nyman

Favourite place to go on holiday

Boston in America

Favourite character in Jacqueline Wilson's books!

Dolphin in *The Illustrated Mum*, though I'm very fond of Biscuits in *Cliffhanger* and *Buried Alive!*

Did you know...?
Ten Fascinating Facts about Jacqueline Wilson

Did you know that Jacqueline Wilson's longest ever book-signing event was six hours?

Did you know that the TV adaptation of *Double Act* featured actress Charlotte Coleman, while the TV version of *The Story of Tracy Beaker* featured her sister, Lisa Coleman?

Did you know that Hay-on-Wye is Jacqueline's favourite town in Britain, because it has about twenty bookshops?

Did you know that Jacqueline Wilson's on-line official fan club (at www.jacquelinewilson.co.uk) has more than 5,000 members?

Did you know that Tanya, one of the main characters in *Bad Girls*, also appears in *Dustbin Baby*?

Did you know that Jacqueline has ridden in a London taxi with the characters from *Girls in Love* painted on it?

Did you know that Jacqueline's daughter used to have a toy rabbit exactly like Radish in *The Suitcase Kid* (and that Jacqueline still has it!)?

Did you know that Nick Sharratt wasn't the original illustrator of Jacqueline Wilson's books (but he has been doing it since 1991)?

Did you know that Jacqueline still writes out the first draft of her novels by hand in a notebook (often writing while travelling by train)?

Did you know that Jacqueline treats herself to a new silver ring or bracelet when each new book is published (that's why she has so many different ones!)?

Here are
the answers!

Answers: Quiz 1

THE ILLUSTRATED MUM

1. Thirty-three
2. Marigold feels that, at thirty-three, she has reached a
    crossroads in her life.
3. Mrs Luft
4. Year Eight
5. Ronnie Churley
6. She is in the kitchen baking masses of cakes and cookies.
7. She says that Tasha has a ballet class.
8. A yellow-and-white daisy chain
9. They make a cake cottage for dormice, like the gingerbread
    house in Hansel and Gretel.
10. Green
11. Bottle Nose
12. Oliver Morris
13. Marigold has brought Star's long-lost father, Micky, back with
    her from the concert.
14. She chooses an orange stripy tiger, with great green eyes.
15. She uses her new credit card.
16. A silk scarf
17. She is upset because Star has just told her that she isn't
    coming home, she's going to live with her dad, in Brighton,
    instead.
18. She rings Mrs Luft downstairs and asks to speak to Dolphin.
19. She calls an ambulance because Marigold has covered
    herself from head to foot with white gloss paint.
20. They met at a swimming pool; he was a swimming
    instructor.

Answers: Quiz 2

DOUBLE ACT

1. Ruby is the elder of the two, by twenty minutes!
2. Ruby finds an old, blank, leather-bound Accounts book in a box, which Dad says they can have for scribbling.
3. Garnet was so nervous that she wet herself on stage!
4. She moves into sheltered housing.
5. He wants to move to the country and set up a bookshop.
6. She runs a bric-à-brac stall in the local shopping arcade.
7. Twinspeak
8. Ruby is travel sick – all over Rose!
9. The Railway Children
10. The Red Bookshop
11. She retrieves the worm and shoves it down the Blob's trousers!
12. A flea
13. She thought Ruby would choose a giraffe, because that has always been the twins' favourite animal.
14. She sells the antique china doll that Gran gave her.
15. Dad
16. 'Snow in Winter'
17 Albert
18. Baldie
19. Little Scrubbing Brush
20. She cooks Garnet's favourite – chicken and chips – and she makes a cake.

Answers: Quiz 3

THE STORY OF TRACY BEAKER

1. 8 May
2. Peter Ingham
3. Lettuce
4. She was taken into care because her mum's Monster Gorilla Boyfriend beat her up.
5. Elaine the Pain
6. Aunty Peggy and Uncle Sid
7. Someone in the Home pokes Bluebell's eyes back inside her head, leaving empty sockets. (Bluebell is a doll!)
8. She discovered that her mum had moved six months before without leaving a forwarding address.
9. They are having a baby of their own, and they know that Tracy got into trouble at her first foster home for shutting a baby in a cupboard.
10. She is writing an article for a magazine about children in care.
11. Louise
12. She dares Justine to say the rudest word she can think of when the vicar comes to visit.
13. She dares Tracy to go out in the garden stark naked.
14. The Quiet Room is where children at the Home are sent to cool down after an outburst of temper.
15. She claims to be suffering from hay fever.
16. Goblinda the Goblin
17. She discovers that Peter is probably going to be fostered, which means he'll be leaving the Home.
18. She suggests that Cam might like to foster her.
19. She gives Tracy her Mickey Mouse pen.
20. She gives Cam's present to Justine Littlewood.

Answers: Quiz 4

THE SUITCASE KID

1. Mulberry Cottage
2. They really contain some very gory video nasties!
3. Bill came to do some painting at Mulberry Cottage.
4. He has three children: Paula, Graham and Katie.
5. She locks herself in the bathroom.
6. Ethel
7. It contains a mulberry tree, just like the one at Mulberry Cottage.
8. Haikus
9. Katie thinks that if she goes to sleep, she might die, like her mum did.
10. Radish falls into a hole in the trunk of the mulberry tree.
11. She runs away because the door of the big house opens and a dark figure comes out into the garden.
12. She ends up back at Mulberry Cottage.
13. The wording says, 'I love you'.
14. Butter-yellow
15. Green
16. The elderly couple have turned the old mulberry into a little tree-house for Radish.
17. Mr and Mrs Peters
18. She gives Andy her very own sewing box.
19. She gives Andy a plaster ornament of Andy Pandy.
20. It is a beautiful wooden toy yacht, which Graham has made for her.

Answers: Quiz 5

THE LOTTIE PROJECT

1. Charlotte Alice Katherine Enright
2. Miss Beckworth is new and wants the class to sit in alphabetical order, until she has got to know all their names.
3. Servants
4. Jamie Edwards
5. He lives in posh Oxford Terrace.
6. She is manageress of a firm dealing in electrical goods.
7. Magic Lands
8. She is a nursery maid.
9. It is in Oxford Terrace and Charlie is terrified that the house might be the one where Jamie Edwards (the class swot) lives.
10. Girls Are Best
11. It is Grandma and Grandpa's pearl wedding anniversary.
12. She has baked an anniversary cake, misspelling the wording on the top. Unfortunately, Grandma points this out in rather a thoughtless way.
13. Jo is really spending time with Robin's dad, Mark, at his house, chatting and watching television with him.
14. Red River Theme Park
15. The Victoria and Albert Museum in London
16. Robin and Charlie see Robin's dad, Mark, kissing Charlie's mum, Jo.
17. He calls because Robin, his five-year-old son, has gone missing.
18. He finds Birdie, Robin's knitted toy robin.
19. Someone snatches baby Freddie from his perambulator in the park and steals him away.
20. She blurts out her troubles to her teacher, Miss Beckworth.

Answers: Quiz 6
THE BED AND BREAKFAST STAR

1. Her mum named her after Elsa the lion, who featured in a book and a film, because Elsa was born with lots of hair, like a lion's mane.
2. She is always telling awful jokes!
3. They stay with Mack's mum.
4. The Royal Hotel
5. They meet Naomi in the Ladies at the Royal Hotel, and she is sitting on the windowsill with her feet in a washbasin, reading a book.
6. Three
7. Nicky, Neil and Nathan
8. Room 608
9. In apricots! (Aargh!)
10. The *Little Women* dustjacket covers a copy of The Cursed Werewolf Runs Wild (unbeknown to Naomi's mother!).
11. Mrs Hoover
12. She writes all sorts of rude things about Mack – 'the Big Twitty Scottish Berk in room 608' – on the wall in the Ladies' loo at the hotel.
13. An old black-and-white portable television
14. She tells them that her mum is a glamorous movie star.
15. He threatens to throw Naomi's family out of the hotel.
16. She discovers that the hotel is on fire.
17. Some of the hotel fire alarms aren't working, so Elsa wakes everyone up by shouting, 'FIRE!'
18. She opens her mouth to speak to the interviewer – and no words come out!
19. Her baseball bomber jacket has a picture of a lion on the back!
20. The Star Hotel

Answers: Quiz 7
VICKY ANGEL

1. They call Vicky and Jade 'The Twins', because they are inseparable.
2. An actress
3. He works on a building site.
4. Vicky's mother, Mrs Waters
5. They live in a second-floor flat on the Oxford estate.
6. Friday
7. She finds a crowd of grieving schoolchildren, and a reporter from the local paper.
8. London
9. She missed the rehearsal for Vicky's funeral.
10. Reasons to Be Cheerful
11. Auburn
12. Jade believes that the ghostly Vicky is telling her not to join the Drama Club.
13. Jade is looking up information about angels on the Internet.
14. Bereavement counselling
15. She tells Jade that she's interested in a young man at work and is thinking about leaving Jade's father.
16. Sam reveals that it's Jade he's always liked, not Vicky.
17. She is a chaplain and a friend of Mrs Cambridge; she has also done a grief counselling course.
18. Mrs Wainwright's five-year-old daughter died of leukaemia.
19. The letter tells Jade that she must give evidence at Vicky's inquest.
20. The ghostly Vicky saves Jade from being run over.

Answers: Quiz 8

BAD GIRLS

1. Kim
2. She runs into the road, into the path of a bus.
3. Toy monkeys
4. Arthur King
5. Carmel
6. Maths
7. King Arthur and the Knights of the Round Table
8. She sees Tanya stealing a green velvet scrunchie.
9. Chess
10. She gives Tanya a propelling pencil that was meant to be for herself.
11. He takes them swimming.
12. Tanya steals a can of hairspray from Boots.
13. She draws a heart tattoo, inside which are entwined the names 'Tanya' and 'Mandy'.
14. Tanya has to move into a children's home.
15. She signs her up for a story-writing session at the local library.
16. Arthur King
17. She has been made redundant from her job.
18. Miss Moseley
19. Bullying
20. Tanya sends Mandy a postcard telling her that she got a supervision order, and now has a nice new foster mum.

Answers: Quiz 9
SECRETS

1. She moves in with her nan because her mum's boyfriend hit her.
2. They argue about India's weight. India is supposed to be on a diet, but she never sticks to it.
3. Miranda
4. The Diary of a Young Girl by Anne Frank
5. Buried (as in Buried Treasure)
6. She is cycling round the Latimer estate on a BMX bike, doing wheelie tricks.
7. Wanda, the Australian au pair, hasn't turned up to collect India from school, so India decides to walk home by herself.
8. Asthma
9. Rita Mitchell
10. Wanda is having a love affair with India's dad.
11. She wants to be a writer, like her heroine, Anne Frank.
12. She bumps into Terry, Treasure's step-father, who caused the scarring on Treasure's forehead by striking her with his belt.
13. She calls it The Official Terry Torture Manual.
14. Britney
15. Mumbly Michael Watkins
16. She lives on the posh Parkfield estate.
17. She suggests that Treasure should hide in the attic room at the top of India's house.
18. She learns that Mumbly Michael Watkins has been arrested on suspicion of abducting Treasure.
19. It is a picture of herself and India enclosed in a heart, with roses all round it.
20. She finds her dad there, looking terrible.

Answers: Quiz 10

Can You Place these Places?

1. Tim and his parents
2. Llanpistyll
3. They find him at the railway station because he is intending to go to Manchester to see his mother.
4. They go to the seaside at Bournemouth.
5. It is crammed with Victorian things which are relevant to her school project.
6. Brighton
7. The Rainbow Tattoo Studio
8. The Latimer estate
9. Australia
10. The job takes place in Amsterdam, in Holland, and they visit the house of Anne Frank there.
11. Canada
12. They move because Elsa's stepfather is offered a job.
13. Kinglea Junior School
14. Chessington World of Adventures
15. She finds an empty house when she is wandering aimlessly round the streets one day, and spends more and more time there, instead of going to school.
16. He is hiding behind the curtain, scrunched up on the window ledge, at the abandoned house.
17. Italy
18. She finds Mabel nestling in her dressing gown on the wardrobe floor – but the cat is dead.
19. He attaches himself to her ankle when she is paddling in the 'witch pond' at her local park.
20. He goes to Paris with his girlfriend.

Answers: Quiz 11

All in the Family!

1. Opal
2. Gran used to work for a posh fashion house, as a dressmaker.
3. Zoë
4. Anne Frank
5. Although Patsy is Treasure's aunt, she is younger than Treasure.
6. India's dad has been accused of embezzling money from his company.
7. Mandy's parents are much older than most of the other mums and dads at school.
8. She committed suicide when Tanya was very young.
9. They met at a school parents' evening — Dad's girlfriend is a teacher at Holly's school.
10. Samantha's dad has left her mum and has a new girlfriend — and they are having a baby.
11. She tells Cam that her mum is probably a film star in Hollywood.
12. Carly Beaker
13. Tracy's social worker passes on a message that Tracy's real mum has been in touch — and wants to see her!
14. Mabel originally belonged to Verity's mum, who is now dead.
15. The posters are asking if anyone has seen Mabel the cat, who has gone missing.
16. Verity has used them to try and preserve Mabel as a cat mummy!
17. Michael's wife is called Meg, and his daughters are Grace and Alice.
18. She is a policewoman.
19. He thinks Tim has turned into a 'Mummy's boy' because Tim is hopeless at every kind of sport.
20. He has to rescue Biscuits, who has climbed over the railings to rescue his lucky mascot, Dog Hog, from the landing stage below.

Answers: Quiz 12
Clues to Clothes and More

1. The ghostly Vicky just imagines what she'd like to wear, and the clothes appear on her, as if by magic.
2. She puts on her old fairy costume.
3. Her hair is braided into little plaits, tied with beads and coloured threads, and she has a diamond stud in her nose.
4. She is upset because she has failed the entrance exam for Marnock Heights, and Garnet has passed.
5. He commands Rebecca to utter his name seven times, and this magical spell makes the sun come out, which dries her dress!
6. Mandy trips over her new shoes and twists her ankle.
7. She is a children's clothes designer.
8. He calls her 'Ginger Twin', because they both have frizzy red hair.
9. She sneaks into Adele's room, plasters her face with Adele's make-up, and then puts on her own mohair sweater, which has 'Tracy' knitted across the front.
10. Her socks have pictures of books on them.
11. A designer T-shirt (with 'chic' written on the front), and a pair of combat trousers.
12. Tanya is a thief: she shoplifts all the accessories.
13. Bright orange
14. Indigo is a trendy fashion shop in which Tanya is caught shoplifting an expensive hand-knitted sweater.
15. She gives Mandy her violet sequin sparkly top.
16. He feels nervous because he is plucking up courage to tell Holly that he likes her and wants her to be his girlfriend!
17. The dress is black, with silver moon and star embroidery.
18. She wears a black velvet jacket, with a sprig of lucky heather pinned to it, and a tartan skirt. Her mum dresses Elsa up like that because Mack is Scottish.
19. A soldier's jacket
20. His arms are covered in tattoos – including one of a bikini-clad lady which he can waggle when he moves his arm muscles!

Answers: Quiz 13
Yum, Yum: All about Food!

1. Sadie is given a chocolate heart with the words, 'Thank you, Sadie!' on the top, in swirly pink icing.
2. She thinks her mum might come to collect her from the Home while she's out with Cam.
3. She gives Tracy a birthday cake with TB spelt out in Smarties on the top.
4. She dares Tracy to tip the spaghetti over her own head – which she does!
5. He has provided himself with a plate of Smarties, arranged in rings of colour to look like a flower.
6. She says it was made of 'cow's nostrils and uddery bits'!
7. Sugar sandwiches
8. Slug stew!
9. She promises him a tin of golden syrup and a packet of biscuits.
10. She makes a model of Mandy out of sweets and wraps it in a cloak of fragrant herbs.
11. The Enormous Mouthful Contest
12. Mrs Angel
13. The message is 'I LIKE YOU', and she gives it to Jamie Edwards.
14. She takes a robin cake that she has made herself.
15. Charlotte Russe
16. Two big, wiggly, green jelly snakes!
17. A big tin of golden syrup!
18. Pizza
19. He chooses the Chocolate Biscuit Choo-Choo Special, comprising an entire packet of chocolate biscuits, sandwiched together with chocolate ice cream, to make a train. It has chocolate button wheels, a flake for a funnel, and cream billowing out along the top for steam.
20. La Terrazza

Answers: Quiz 14
Playing Games

1. The Fun Run Friday Club
2. Mr Lorrimer
3. She was at an aerobics class.
4. The Tigers
5. Abseiling
6. Kelly drops the troll doll in the water, but Tim rescues it.
7. French cricket
8. He likes fishing best, because you just sit there doing very little – and then you eat the fish you've caught!
9. He plays the 'burying Tim in the sand' game – to get his own back on Tim for going off with Kelly!
10. New Barnes Leisure Pool
11. He enjoyed pen and paper games, like noughts and crosses.
12. He is playing football (instead of being at school) and accidentally kicks the ball at Tracy as she comes round a corner.
13. She is planning a weekend at the races with her latest boyfriend.
14. Football and his dad used to go to a match every Saturday, but his dad hasn't turned up recently, because he has a new girlfriend.
15. He suggests that, as football is one of Claire's strengths, she should kick an imaginary ball at The Monster video image that is frightening her.
16. David Beckham
17. They had rows because Samantha's dad always flirted with the other ladies he met at badminton, tennis and swimming.
18. She uses Katie's Watch with Mother video tape, featuring Andy Pandy.
19. She makes them run round and round the playground, without stopping, for the entire lesson!
20. Swimming (Jacqueline swims fifty lengths at her local pool before breakfast every morning!)

Answers: Quiz 15
TV, Radio and the Theatre

1. *The Story of Tracy Beaker*
2. Susan Tully
3. *Double Act*
4. *The Lottie Project*
5. The Polka Children's Theatre, in Wimbledon, London
6. Jacqueline was voted the fourth Most Popular Children's Author in the poll.
7. *Double Act*
8. Tracy Beaker
9. *Children in Crisis*
10. He thinks Elsa's interview is unsuitable because all she does is tell a series of jokes; the director wants an interview about how awful life in a bed-and-breakfast hotel is.
11. *Children of Courage*
12. *The Twins at St Clare's*
13. Ruby performs with great confidence, but Garnet dries up completely and feels hugely embarrassed.
14. Marnock Heights
15. *The Tracy Beaker Experience*
16. *Blue Peter* (Alexander has drawn a picture of the presenters on the front of the pretend TV)
17. The actress, Sharon Stone
18. They see Treasure's mum and awful stepfather on the news, appealing for information in connection with Treasure's disappearance.
19. *A Child's Right to Choose*
20. The speaking machine on Natasha's wheelchair performs the chorus to their song about the Worry Website.

Answers: Quiz 16

School Life

1. Mr Harrison
2. He finds them a book about dolphins, full of pictures and information.
3. Jamilla is Garnet's 'Sheepdog', so-called because she shows Garnet where everything is at her new boarding school.
4. Miss Jeffreys
5. She is a fictional classmate of India's, whom India pretends to visit when she's really seeing Treasure, who lives on a run-down estate.
6. Treasure's nan is in the headmistress's office, trying to locate India, to see if she knows where Treasure is.
7. She makes Charlie write out *five* formal letters of apology – all different – at home that night!
8. Jamie Edwards
9. Charlie
10. The Ancient Egyptians
11. Miss Smith
12. She suggests that Verity should make a special book about Mabel, to include photos and recollections about the happy times they had together.
13. She has to write a holiday diary.
14. Tracy hit Roxanne Green, because Roxanne made rude comments about Tracy being born out of wedlock.
15. It is PE – because the other boys laugh at him in the showers!
16. He threatens to send him to boarding school – where Alexander will *really* be bullied and will have to learn to stand up for himself.
17. Gherkin
18. Mr Speed
19. Miss Morgan *used* to be Holly's favourite teacher – until she started going out with Holly's dad!
20. She complains to Mrs Edwards about the bullying to which Mandy has been subjected by Kim, Melanie and Sarah.

Answers: Quiz 17
What's in a Name?

1. Fatboy Sam
2. Vicky is dead and Jade imagines that she sees a ghostly Vicky with hair shining, like an angel's halo. This 'ghost' tells Jade to call her 'Vicky Angel'.
3. Sporty, Scary, Baby and Posh
4. Dustbin
5. It means 'truth', and the name suits Verity because she tries very hard to tell the truth – although sometimes that proves a bit difficult!
6. Sir Algernon Honeypot
7. Piles!
8. Prickle-Head and Pinch-Face
9. The Boss
10. Jeremy Treadgold
11. Andy Pandy
12. Zen and Crystal
13. Rebecca Cockgoldde
14. It is the correct Latin term for the common toad!
15. She is a doll with long golden curls and a blue lacy dress, given to Tracy by her mum.
16. Mrs Vomit Bagley (or Mrs V. B.)
17. She calls it the 'Bat Cave' (because Tracy has chosen black for the colour scheme).
18. She is the pretty and glamorous imaginary girl that Mandy wishes she really was.
19. He is called 'Wetty Willie', because his classmates have discovered that he wets the bed.
20. Twinkle

Answers: Quiz 18
Everybody's Favourites

1. White lilies
2. Baby Pillow
3. Her stepfather, Mack the Smack
4. Blood red!
5. Smarties
6. *The Wizard of Oz*
7. It is Camilla, because Tracy had a little friend by that name in a previous Children's Home; it is also Cam's proper name.
8. *Snow White*
9. Her least favourite colour is slime green – because it reminds her of The Monster, a frightening video nasty she has watched.
10. Red – because rubies are red, and so are garnets!
11. Drama
12. He doesn't have a favourite sport – he HATES them all!
13. Butterscotch
14. Emerald City
15. Olivia Orang-Utan
16. *The Wizard of Oz*
17. Child-minder!
18. Blood-red raspberry fruit gums!
19. Boston, in America. Jacqueline likes this place because there are lots of great bookshops, art galleries and restaurants.
20. Nick Sharratt

Answers: Quiz 19

Extra-tricky for Truly Dedicated Fans!

1. Nick Sharratt
2. *Jackie* (of course!)
3. *Double Act* and *Buried Alive!* have two illustrators (Nick Sharratt and Sue Heap) because the main characters, Ruby and Garnet (in *Double Act*) and Tim and Biscuits (in *Buried Alive!*), are supposed to have drawn the pictures themselves.
4. They both enjoy line-dancing!
5. Latchmere Primary School and Coombe Girls Secondary School
6. She receives at least 200 fan letters a week!
7. They are all crime novels.
8. *The Illustrated Mum*
9. It must be July — two months after Tracy's birthday (8 May).
10. It is the one where Football dares Tracy to take off her knickers, climb up the fir tree outside the empty house, and hang them on the top branch, like a Christmas decoration! (*The Dare Game*)
11. Manic depression
12. This is the motto of Ruby and Garnet, the twins in *Double Act*.
13. Mandy (*Bad Girls*)
14. Cussop
15. Gorselea, in Sussex
16. They are a sensitive subject because Ruby sold hers at a car-boot sale for £20, but Rose helped Garnet sell hers at an auction for £600!
17. She gives him Jane Eyre by Charlotte Brontë, because it is 'by a Charlotte, from a Charlotte!'
18. *Vicky Angel*
19. Bastet
20. *For the Dimwits, who aren't dim at all, but are very witty.*

Answers: Quiz 20

All about Jacqueline Wilson!

1. Bath
2. Kingston-upon-Thames, in Surrey
3. She was nine years old.
4. None
5. About 15,000!
6. Fruit, cakes, chips and ice cream (but not all together!)
7. 17 December
8. Sagittarius
9. She has one grown-up daughter, called Emma.
10. Black and silver
11. Ten
12. She worked in publishing, and then as a magazine journalist.
13. Dolphin, in *The Illustrated Mum*, or maybe Biscuits in *Cliffhanger* and *Buried Alive!*, or maybe Tracy Beaker ('although she's totally outrageous')!
14. Jane Eyre (in Charlotte Brontë's novel)
15. Over six million!
16. *Girls in Love, Girls under Pressure, Girls Out Late and Girls in Tears*
17. They both carry a lucky rabbit mascot called Radish!
18. There isn't one – they're all very untidy!
19. *Double Act*
20. The Smarties Prize, the Children's Book of the Year Award and the Sheffield Book of the Year Award.

SCORING

Now that you have completed the quizzes, it's time to tot up the points! Score one point for each correct answer, or two for each correct answer in the Extra-tricky Quiz for Truly Dedicated Fans. (It's OK to award one point for an Extra-tricky question that's half right!) Keep a record of your scores in the grids on the following pages – and see how you get on compared with your friends!

Quiz Number	Names					
1						
2						
3						
4						
5						
6						
7						
8						
9						
10						
11						
12						
13						
14						
15						
16						
17						
18						
19						
20						

In case you need more scoring space…
 Remember you could do the quizzes more than once – will you improve each time?

Names

Quiz Number						
1						
2						
3						
4						
5						
6						
7						
8						
9						
10						
11						
12						
13						
14						
15						
16						
17						
18						
19						
20						

Quiz Number	Names					
1						
2						
3						
4						
5						
6						
7						
8						
9						
10						
11						
12						
13						
14						
15						
16						
17						
18						
19						
20						

Quiz Number	Names					
1						
2						
3						
4						
5						
6						
7						
8						
9						
10						
11						
12						
13						
14						
15						
16						
17						
18						
19						
20						
Average Score						

☆ Assess your score ☆

Let's see how you did! Are you a *Jacqueline Wilson Quiz Book* champ or a chump?

An Average of 16–20 points per quiz (or 31–40 Extra–tricky points)

Congratulations! It is clear that you are highly intelligent, well-informed, widely-read and a truly dedicated Jacqueline Wilson fan! You deserve all the Smarties in the tube for being the smartiest pants in the laundry basket. You probably know more about Jacqueline Wilson than Jacqueline Wilson does!

An Average of 11–15 points per quiz (or 21–30 Extra–tricky points)

Not bad at all! You weren't quite up there with the eggheads, but you're certainly no featherbrain! Our guess is that you enjoy a jolly good read, but your little brother or sister sometimes rips out the odd page – which is why you can't quite remember ALL the answers!

An Average of 6–10 points per quiz (or 11–20 Extra-tricky points)

It doesn't sound like you've really been concentrating! Or maybe it's just that you haven't read the books for a while, so your memory is a bit hazy. You may not be a quiz champion but you probably have a winning smile to make up for it!

An Average of 0–5 points per quiz (or 0–10 Extra-tricky points)

Well, you win the Bird Brain Booby Prize for having the shortest memory on record! Of course, there's always the possibility that you were asleep during the quiz!

WRITE YOUR OWN JACQUELINE WILSON QUIZ

Finished all the quizzes in the book and feel like your brain is bursting with fascinating facts about your favourite author? Why not have a go at writing your very own Jacqueline Wilson quiz? You can try and trick your best friends with the most fiendish and obscure questions that you can think up. Write the questions here and then try them on your mates!

Don't miss:

The Jacqueline Wilson Address Book

Never forget a friend's number again!

Keep all the names, numbers and addresses
you need organized in the mega-useful,
first-ever *Jacqueline Wilson Address Book*.
Illustrated throughout by Nick Sharratt, this
is a must-have for all dedicated fans.

Doubleday